# ENCHANTING
# BANGKOK

## MICK SHIPPEN

# Contents

*Above:* The Royal Barge Procession making its way down the Chao Phraya River to celebrate the 85th birthday of King Bhumibol Adulyadej.

*Above left:* A traditional Thai dancer at the Erawan Shrine.

*Opposite:* Sukhumvit Road, at the heart of Bangkok, lit up at night.

*Title page:* Wat Arun on the west bank of the Chao Phraya River features a distinctive 'prang' or Khmer-style chedi.

# Chapter 1: The City of Angels

Modern-day Bangkok is an assault on the senses. The heaving metropolis has experienced decades of sustained and uncontrolled development yet it retains an allure that makes it one of Asia's most exciting and exotic cities.

Bangkok's life and landscape were transformed during the boom time of the early 90s when the city was the beating heart of a roaring 'tiger economy'. Skyscrapers quickly rose to overshadow golden temple spires, streets became gridlocked and the nightlife gained a reputation for being spicier than Thailand's chilli-laced cuisine. For a brief period, the chaos meant that Bangkok was viewed by tourists just as a two-day stopover on the way to Chiang Mai in the mountainous north or to idyllic islands in the south. Today, however, the city is one of Asia's most popular travel destinations in its own right. Here, visitors are immediately immersed in a world that is not only uniquely Thai but also uniquely Bangkok; an intriguing fusion enriched by the glories of the past and enlivened by an idiosyncratic take on contemporary culture.

Yes, it remains as chaotic as ever and the streets are still clogged with traffic but Bangkok's charms are many. Officially the city's population is 11 million but the true figure is closer to 14 million. Bangkok has always acted as a magnet, attracting villagers from the provinces in search of work and a better life. It is this, in part, that has imbued the city with a special flavour.

Thailand's one constant and stabilizing influence down through the centuries is Buddhism. In Bangkok alone there are 700 Buddhist temples, many regarded as historically significant sites, or in the case of the Grand Palace and the Temple of the Emerald Buddha, the spiritual heart of the nation.

**Above:** The former Russian Embassy on Sathorn Road dates from 1888. Today it is hemmed in between gleaming skyscrapers. Recently restored, the building is now part of W Hotel.

**Opposite:** Bangkok's clean and efficient elevated rapid transit system, the BTS SkyTrain, whisks travellers above the traffic jams from 6 a.m. to midnight.

Down a labyrinth of narrow streets in the old district and in one of the largest and most vibrant Chinatowns in the world, visitors can still catch a glimpse of a life that moves at its own sedate pace. There are also pockets of calm and tranquillity to be discovered that reveal the city's more spiritual side.

The pace and the effect of change elsewhere in the city, however, cannot be underestimated. Many neighbourhoods have been levelled to make way for temples to consumerism and unrestrained excess. In recent years Bangkok has become just as well known for its palatial malls as it is for palaces. Add chic nightclubs, a trendy dining scene, luxurious hotels and apartments, and a continually expanding rapid transit system to the mix and Bangkok is clearly a city on the move.

With typically beguiling charm, the Thais don't refer to the capital city as Bangkok. To them it is simply *Krung Thep*, a welcome abbreviation of 'Krungthep Mahanakhon Amorn Rattanakosin Mahintara Yudthaya Mahadilok Pohp Noparat Rajathanee Bureerom Udomrajniwes Mahasatarn Amorn Pimarn Avaltarnsatit Sakatattiya Visanukram Prasit'. This translates as 'The city of angels, the great city, the eternal jewel city, the impregnable city of God Indra, the grand capital of the world endowed with nine precious gems, the happy city, abounding in an enormous Royal Palace that resembles the heavenly abode where reigns the reincarnated god, a city given by Indra and built by Vishnukam'.

A grand and outdated title it may be but today's Bangkok is deserving of an equally praiseworthy string of superlatives and many days of a traveller's time.

*Right:* Thailand's main artery, the Chao Phraya River, flows from the north through the centre of Bangkok.

# Geography and Climate

Thailand comprises four geographical regions; central, northeast, north and south. Metropolitan Bangkok is situated in the lower central region within the basin of the Chao Phraya River, the country's major waterway that runs from north to south, flowing through Bangkok before spilling into the Gulf of Thailand, 30 km (19 miles) south of the city.

**Opposite:** The Rama IX Bridge, named in honour of King Bhumibol Adulyadej's 60th birthday.

**Below:** The skyline is constantly changing and features many striking, modern buildings.

The Bangkok Metropolitan Area is a vast sprawling city encompassing 50 districts in an area of 1,568.7 km² (606 sq miles), with Greater Bangkok extending to 7,762 km² (2,997 sq miles). Held within a loop of the Chao Phraya River, Ratanakosin Island, often referred to as Old Bangkok, sits on the eastern bank and is home to the city's finest historic landmarks, government buildings and museums. Chinatown is also located in Old Bangkok. Since the days when The Oriental Hotel opened in 1876, the riverbank in the area of Taksin Bridge has always attracted hotels, and today, luxury apartments, restaurants and shopping complexes.

Central Bangkok is generally regarded as the area around Silom and Sukhumvit Roads. Both districts are renowned as the main tourist areas because of the high concentration of department stores, hotels and serviced apartments, restaurants and the city's colourful nightlife. Along with Sathorn and Ploenchit, Silom and Sukhumvit

also form the central business district. In recent years, the location of BTS Skytrain and MRT underground stations has helped once overlooked neighbourhoods, such as Thonglor and Ekamai, develop into fashionable hotspots known for their restaurants, boutiques and upmarket apartments.

The nearby provinces of Chonburi, Ayutthaya, Samut Sakhon, Phetchaburi and Phrachuap Kirikhan are popular as weekend escapes for Bangkokians.

Bangkok is a year-round destination with a humid, three-season, monsoonal climate. Temperatures range from a low of 28°C (82°F) to a high of 38°C (100°F). The most agreeable temperatures can be enjoyed in the cooler months of November, December and January. The hottest months are March and April when temperatures soar to 38°C (100°F) and drop very little in the evening. The rainy season begins in May and peaks in late September and October when the brief but heavy downpours are a daily occurrence.

# A Brief History of Bangkok

Prior to the creation of Bangkok, Ayutthaya was the capital of the Kingdom then known as Siam. In 1767, troops from neighbouring Myanmar attacked the city and won a fierce two-year battle during which manuscripts, religious sculptures and temples were destroyed.

*Below:* Myths and legends of the epic Thai 'Ramakien', which is derived from the Hindu 'Ramayana', painted on the walls of Wat Pho, the Temple of the Reclining Buddha.

Following their defeat, the Thais fled Ayutthaya and under the rule of King Taksin (1767–1782) established a new capital further south at Thonburi on the banks of the Chao Phraya River. However, with the Kingdom still reeling from the effects of war, Thonburi's status was short-lived, collapsing in disorder at the end of Taksin's reign after just 15 years.

## Across the Chao Phraya

In 1782, Rama I was crowned the first king of the Chakri dynasty. He decided to move the capital across the Chao Phraya River to Bang Makawk (later known to foreign traders simply as Bangkok), a site of just four square kilometres (one and a half square miles) but blessed with

*Left: A beautiful painting on the wall of an ancient Bangkok temple depicting Buddha giving a sermon to monks. Today, Buddhism remains at the heart of Thai society.*

*Below: A statue of King Mongkut (Rama VI) in front of Lumpini Park. Educated in England at Sandhurst and Oxford, he ruled from 1910 until his death in 1925. He is credited with introducing the western calendar and surnames.*

greater natural defences against invaders. On the auspicious date of 6th May, 1782, construction of a royal residence, throne halls and temples began, many built by artisans who had survived the sacking of Ayutthaya. The area's river defences were also further strengthened with the excavation of canals and the construction of thick walls to form Koh Ratanakosin, or Ratanakosin Island, the seat of royalty and government, and home to the Grand Palace, Wat Pho (the Temple of the Reclining Buddha), the Golden Mount, Sanam Luang Park, and many more important cultural sites. The canal system which Rama I began continued to be expanded up until the mid-19th century and was eventually so extensive that foreign emissaries dubbed Bangkok 'the Venice of the East'.

It was during the reign of Rama III (1824–1851) that Bangkok began to develop trade with China and increase domestic agricultural production. Under King Mongkut, Rama IV (1851–1868), diplomatic relations were established with European nations in a move that was seen as a skilful way to avoid colonization. In 1861 European diplomats and merchants petitioned the king requesting that more roadways be built to accommodate horse-drawn carriages.

These included Thanon Charoen Krung, also known as New Road, a 10-km (6-mile) stretch running alongside the Chao Phraya River and through today's Chinatown. Successive kings continued the road-building efforts which included Thanon Ratchadamnoen, a broad promenade running east to west through Koh Ratanakosin. Built under the orders of King Chulalongkorn, Rama V (1868–1910), the road is said to have been modelled on the Champs Elysées. Rama V also pushed ahead with the modernization of Thailand's legal and administrative systems, and the construction of railways; moves that fuelled the further development of Bangkok. Most of the original city wall was also demolished, save for two forts, a large gate and a section of the wall which were preserved. In 1882, Bangkok's centenary was marked by the completion of the royal temple, Wat Phra Kaew, the Temple of the Emerald Buddha.

## European Influence

By 1892 Bangkok had a postal service, electric trams running along Thanon Charoen Krung and, by the end of the century, the first stretch of the State Railway running from Bangkok 76 km (47 miles) north to the former capital of Ayutthaya. Rama V's love of all things European could be clearly seen in French-style bridges and the splendid Renaissance-influenced Ananta Samakhom Throne Hall, designed by Italian architects, Mario Tamagno and Annibale Rigotti.

Public works continued under the reign of Rama VI (1910-1925) who established Chulalongkorn University in 1916 and gave the people Lumpini Park, which remains Bangkok's largest green space. In 1937 Bangkok was divided into two municipalities, Krung Thep and Thonburi,

*Left:* The ornate dome of the Ananta Samakhom Throne Hall was commissioned by King Chulalongkorn (Rama V). Constructed in the Italian Renaissance and Neo-Classical style, it was completed in 1910.

*Opposite:* Asiatique, an expansive upmarket riverside night bazaar and dining zone, draws on the area's rich history of maritime trade. The site was once owned by the East Asiatic Company Ltd, a Danish shipping company that began trading with Thailand in 1898.

both encompassing around 96 km² (37 sq miles) but at the time almost four-fifths of the city's population resided in Krung Thep.

Following World War II, Bangkok began to experience rapid and uncontrolled growth. During the late 40s and 50s bridges were built over the Chao Phraya River, and many of the city's canals were filled in for roads. During the Vietnam War from 1962 to 1975, Thailand allowed America to establish several bases within the country and it was during this period that Bangkok became renowned as an R&R destination for soldiers.

In recent years, Bangkok and its people have endured political turmoil that has included coups, and months of street protests, and catastrophic flooding, all of which have been borne with typical resilience and good humour by the city's population.

# The People

As the economic powerhouse of Thailand, Bangkok attracts people from all over the country. The disarmingly friendly population make Bangkok one of Asia's safest and most welcoming cities.

Bangkok has one of the most homogenous populations of any city in Southeast Asia with Thais accounting for 81%. The Chinese have a long history of migration to Thailand that dates back to the 16th century and today Bangkok has a strong Thai-Chinese presence that is estimated to be around 15% (although some claim that it could be in excess of 30%). They are also one of the region's most well-integrated groups. During the reign of Rama VI many Chinese were granted citizenship and adopted Thai surnames. Thai-Chinese also dominate Bangkok's business sector from small noodle and rice shops to banking, major manufacturing and retailing. Twenty-one of the last 29 prime ministers have also been of Chinese descent.

There are several Mon communities in Bangkok. Originally from Myanmar, the first settlers came here as long ago as the 16th century. Many of the Mon were renowned for their pottery-making skills and established workshops on Koh Kred, a manmade island in the Chao Phraya River. Although the pots they make today are commercial, a small museum on the island displays a collection of their traditional work in the form of beautiful earthenware water jars. There is also a large Mon community at Phraphadaeng.

Bangkok has a small but vibrant Indian community that can be traced back to the 1860s. Today it is centred on Phahurat, a district known for its thriving textile trade and

*Right:* This elaborate gate marks the eastern entrance to Bangkok's Chinatown, which is the largest in the country. The Chinese have had a huge influence on Thai culture and commerce.

*Left:* Office workers on Silom Road heading out for a lunch of street food. Bangkok is Thailand's commercial capital but the city's professional class and business owners are predominantly Thai-Chinese.

*Below:* The colour and character on the streets of Bangkok come from the people of the northeast or 'Issan'. They find work as labourers, taxi drivers, hotel staff and street vendors.

Indian restaurants. Many of the most successful Indian families are involved in the hospitality business and own high-profile hotels in central Sukhumvit.

There is a Middle Eastern community based around Nana on Sukhumvit Road and Bangkok also has a sizeable expat community including Chinese, Koreans, Japanese and Europeans.

# Bangkok people at work and play

Driven by the Thais' natural entrepreneurial spirit and long working hours, Bangkok enjoys its status as one of Asia's most successful commercial centres. However, it is also a city that refuses to take itself too seriously. Life in Bangkok is infused with the distinctly Thai spirit of *sanook* or fun. To the lighthearted Thais, enjoyment is a guiding principle to the point that seriousness is almost frowned upon. Equally important is the *mai pen rai* or 'never mind' attitude. Disappointment and annoyances will often be simply dismissed with this frequently heard phrase.

# Religion

Thailand is the world's largest Buddhist nation and the only country in the world where the constitution declares that the monarch must be Buddhist. Reflecting the national figure, Bangkok's population is 95% Buddhist.

Religion pervades all aspects of life in the city, from grand royal ceremonies to early morning alms-giving and the blessing of a new business or car. To experience Buddhism firsthand, a visit to a temple is an essential and insightful experience. On one of the many religious days, such as Visakha Bucha Day, which commemorates the birth, enlightenment and the passing of Buddha, thousands of Thais can be seen making donations, lighting incense and candles, and offering flowers at the feet of golden Buddha images.

*Above:* At Chinese New Year, Thai-Chinese go en-masse to temples and pay respect to the Buddha. The air is filled with incense as they line up to give offerings and seek blessings from monks.

*Right:* Asoke Road in central Bangkok packed with hundreds of Buddhist monks and worshippers at a mass alms giving ceremony to mark the 2,600th anniversary of the Buddha's enlightenment.

*Right:* Buddhist monks gathered in central Bangkok to pray and receive alms from followers.

*Left:* At the Erawan Shrine it is common to see Buddhists release birds from cages as an act of merit making.

*Below:* Thai Buddhism borrows strongly from animism and spirit houses can be seen outside homes and businesses. Offerings of food, water, flowers and incense are made each day to placate mischievous spirits.

Thai Buddhism is infused with animist beliefs that predate the arrival of Buddhism in the region. In Bangkok, superstition and the belief in the spirit world are an integral part of everyday life and worship. This is most visible in the form of the numerous spirit houses outside homes and businesses built to placate the spirits that were disturbed when the land was dug for construction. Faith in the power of protection from the spirits also extends to the use of Buddhist amulets worn around the neck and religious tattoos.

Bangkok lacks the diversity of other Southeast Asian cities but there is a history of regional immigration and there are several long-established Muslim communities, many of which are located on the banks of the Chao Phraya River and beside canals. It is estimated that there are 260,000 Thai-speaking Muslims in various communities of 150-200 households which are served by their own schools and mosques. Historically, many of the city's Muslims came to Bangkok via southern Thailand and Malaysia while others came from Cham communities in Cambodia, as well as Afghanistan, Bangladesh, Myanmar, India, Pakistan, Iran and China.

Bangkok is also home to a small Roman Catholic Thai-Vietnamese community at Ban Yuan in the Samsen Road area of the city, an Arab neighbourhood in the Nana area of Sukhumvit Road, and Sikhs in Phahurat.

# Street Eats

Food vendors are such a ubiquitous part of life in Bangkok that it is hard to imagine the city without them. Tens of thousands of street stalls can be found all over the metropolis, making it one of the most exciting places in the world to eat. Hungry Bangkokians grab a curbside breakfast, and at lunch times and after work street stalls swarm with office staff; the air is filled with the irresistible aroma of dozens of different dishes, the choking waft of stir-fried chillies, lemongrass-scented soups and charcoal-grilled meats.

Although the traditional Chinese noodle or chicken-rice stall is still very much part of Bangkok's culinary landscape, the majority of the footpath food hawkers are economic migrants from Issan, the impoverished northeast of Thailand. During the booming 90s resilient and hardworking Issan people moved to the city in droves to work as taxi drivers or as labourers on construction sites, bringing with them their distinctive music, culture, and, of course, food.

**Above:** A fruit vendor on the streets of Bangkok. The city is a haven for food lovers with stalls every few metres offering a bewildering and enticing array of delicious dishes.

**Right:** A roadside vendor cooks up a stir-fry in Chinatown. The area is known for its excellent street food and attracts hordes of diners in the evenings.

**Above:** Bangkok is one of the world's most exciting cities for food. Visitors can embark on a culinary adventure infused with new and enticing flavours.

**Left:** Thailand may be known for classic dishes such as 'tom yam' and 'green curry' but there is so much more to discover. Clean and freshly cooked, street food is an essential ingredient of any trip to Bangkok.

Far from egalitarian, Thailand's hierarchical social structure meant that Bangkok's elite and middle classes dismissed Issan as 'baan nok', the 'back-of-beyond'. In the not-too-distant past the rich coconut milk curries of central Thailand and the food of Chinese immigrants dominated the diet of Bangkok Thais. But when adaptable Issan workers established street stalls selling northeastern delights across the entire city, their simple yet spicy food proved a hit with everyone. *Somtam*, a raw papaya salad, is the best-known dish from the northeast and if anything could now be considered the national dish of Thailand it is this fiery favourite. Made in a large pestle and mortar called a *krok*, *somtam* sellers pepper the streets of Bangkok; the familiar *pok, pok, pok* sound made as the dish is mixed alerting passersby to their presence. Accompanied by *gai yang* (grilled chicken), sticky rice, steamed vegetables and dipping sauces, it's a menu of delights that can be found on every street.

Despite the popularity of street vendors, their profession is far from secure. Over the years a succession of city governors has attempted to control their trade, blaming them for contributing to traffic problems or stating that they are a nuisance to pedestrians. Although the threatened legislation has often resulted in compromise, some years ago Mondays were declared a vendor-free day, and when international dignitaries visit Thailand stall owners are often banned from certain areas in order to 'clean up the city and create a good impression'. It is at such times that it becomes apparent just how much the city's character is defined by these remarkable roadside chefs.

**This page:** 'Somtam' is considered Thailand's national dish and is loved by everyone. The dish of raw papaya and red hot chillies is made with a mortar and pestle by street vendors, and often accompanied by grilled chicken and sticky rice.

**Above:** On Mangkom (Dragon) Road in Chinatown, diners tuck into a simple meal of curry and rice at the popular vendor's stall known as Jek Pui. It was started more than 50 years ago by the present owner's father. Even the lack of tables doesn't discourage customers.

**Left:** Dining street-side in Bangkok presents visitors with unfamiliar dishes. Just tuck in and enjoy new tastes, textures and ingredients. Street food is not only delicious, it's very cheap.

# Festivals and Celebrations

Thailand's major annual festivals, such as Songkran (New Year) in April and Loy Kratong in November are celebrated with typical Thai enthusiasm and *sanook* across Bangkok. There are also several other distinctive events to experience throughout the year.

## Chinese New Year

At Chinese New Year, which falls in January or February, Bangkok's huge Chinese community in the Yaowarat district holds an annual fair lasting several days. Chinese music, lion dancing, local cultural performances, Chinese opera and fireworks, dining in the street, and making merit through prayer and donations at the district's many famous temples are all part of this fabulously colourful celebration.

**Opposite below:** *At Chinese New Year it becomes apparent just how much the city is run by the Thai-Chinese community. Bangkok practically grinds to a halt for several days as many close their businesses for an annual holiday, enjoy celebratory feasts and make merit at temples.*

**Above:** *Day and night, temples in Chinatown are filled with worshippers who light candles and incense, and make offerings to ensure good fortune for the coming year.*

**Above right:** *Chinese opera, or 'ngiew', in Thailand dates back more than three centuries. There are several troupes and performances can be seen at Chinese New Year.*

# Ploughing Ceremony

In May, a traditional Ploughing Ceremony is held to mark the start of the country's rice-growing season. The elaborate ceremony is thought to have originated over 700 years ago during the Sukhothai period. Officials dressed in traditional costume lead two sacred white oxen across Sanam Luang Park in Bangkok, turning over the soil with a royal plough. The oxen are offered grass, rice, sesame seeds, soy beans, corn, water and whiskey, and depending on which the beasts choose a prediction is made for the year's rainfall and rice crop. Following the ceremony rice is cast onto the ground and onlookers scramble to collect the grains that are considered sacred.

*This page:* Rarely held, the Royal Barge Procession is a tradition that transports viewers to a bygone era. Thousands throng the banks of the Chao Phraya to get a glimpse of the colourful event.

# Royal Barge Procession

The Royal Barge Procession is one of the country's grandest ceremonies but is rarely held, being reserved for auspicious occasions. The ancient tradition, which is thought to date back to the 14th century and the Ayutthaya period died out in 1932 with the dissolution of Thailand's absolute monarchy. However, it was revived in 1957 by His Late Majesty King Bhumibol Adulyadej, the ninth king of the Chakri Dynasty and the longest reigning monarch in Thai history. Since this time the event has only been held on 17 occasions, the last being in 2019 to celebrate the coronation of King Vajiralongkorn (Rama X). The grand spectacle includes 51 historic barges and the 44-m (144-foot) royal barge, known as the Narai Song Suban, which was constructed for King Bhumibol in 1994, all manned by

2,082 specially trained oarsmen. The procession travels along the Chao Phraya, also known as the River of Kings, carrying the revered Buddha image, Phra Buddha Sihing, and members of the royal family, stopping at Wat Arun where they present offerings of saffron robes, food and other necessities to the monks. At other times, the collection of exquisitely carved boats can be seen at the Royal Barges Museum at Bangkok Noi.

# Makha Bucha

Makha Bucha is one of Thailand's most important religious festivals and a national holiday. Held on the full moon of the third lunar month, it commemorates the day when 1,250 monks gathered spontaneously to hear the Buddha preach. The festival is celebrated across Thailand with candlelit processions. In Bangkok, the Golden Mount is one of the most popular places to go.

*This page:* On the evening of Makha Bucha, Buddhist monks gather at the Golden Mount for prayer and candlelit processions. Every other temple in the city also marks the occasion in the same way.

# Vegetarian Festival

Each year in Bangkok's Chinatown the community holds a Vegetarian Festival. The event begins on the first evening of the ninth lunar month, usually in October, and continues until the ninth evening. The festival attracts huge crowds who according to tradition must adhere to ten rules which include abstaining from eating meat, drinking alcohol and having sex. The food markets across the city sell vegetarian food and temples hold ceremonies to honour the gods. In Chinatown, dragon and lion dances are held in the streets and intriguing performances of *ngiew* or traditional Chinese opera can be seen.

# Chapter 2: Spiritual Bangkok

**B**angkok is home to some of Asia's most important Buddhist temples. From the glorious Wat Phra Kaew within the grounds of the Grand Palace to the enigmatic beauty of the enormous Reclining Buddha at Wat Pho, the city skyline is pierced with golden chedi spires.

## Grand Palace and Wat Phra Kaew

**These pages:** *Wat Phra Kaew or the Temple of the Emerald Buddha (right) in the Grand Palace (above) is one of the highlights of a Bangkok tour. Completed in 1784, it is Thailand's most important and sacred temple. The main building houses a 70-cm (27 ½-in) Emerald Buddha. The figure holds great significance for the Thai people and is highly revered. The golden robe draped around the Buddha is changed three times a year by King Vajiralongkorn. Golden chedis within the compound feature colourful, mythical demon guardians (below).*

# Amulet Market

**Right:** The streets on the north side of the Grand Palace are a popular place for buying Buddhist amulets, charms and talismen. During the reign of Rama IV, amulets were made to be distributed to the faithful. Today, the small clay tablets can fetch very high prices depending on the rarity of the style, the status of the monk who blessed it and the supernatural powers it is said to give the wearer.

# Wat Saket and the Golden Mount

***Left and opposite below:***
Wat Saket's major feature is the Golden Mount, a man-made hill constructed during the reign of Rama III in the 1800s and topped by a Lanka-style chedi covered in gold leaf. From the chedi visitors can enjoy panoramic views of historic Bangkok.

# Wat Pho

**These pages:** The Reclining Buddha at Wat Pho (opposite below) is one of the most impressive statues in Thailand. The 46 m (151 feet) long and 15 m (49 feet) high figure was constructed in 1832 during the reign of Rama III. Designed to illustrate the passing of the Buddha into nirvana, the enormous feet feature mother-of-pearl inlay decoration showing the 108 auspicious characteristics of the true Buddha.

The inner and outer galleries at Wat Pho are lined with 788 Buddha images, the largest collection in Thailand. Wat Pho is also a centre for the teaching of traditional Thai medicine and massage. Rama III instructed that the temple should become a centre of learning and had traditional knowledge inscribed on stone slabs.

# Wat Suthat and Sao Ching Cha

**Opposite page:** Wat Suthat, on Bamrung Muang Road, is renowned for the impressive murals in the main chapel of the temple that date from the 19th century. In the main hall, a 700-year-old bronze Buddha image contains the ashes of Rama VIII, uncle of the current king.

**Right:** The distinctive giant swing outside the temple, known as Sao Ching Cha, was once used in Brahmanic ceremonies. The surrounding area is also known for selling Buddha images and religious paraphernalia.

# Erawan Shrine

**These pages:** Located at the intersection of Ratchadamri and Ploenchit Roads, the Erawan Shrine is a colourful spot where Bangkokians come to pray. The busy shrine was built in 1956 to appease the evil spirits that were said to be dogging construction of the original Erawan Hotel (now replaced by the Grand Hyatt Erawan). Once the shrine opened, accidents that had plagued the building site were said to have ceased. Dedicated to Brahma, the four-faced golden image here attracts thousands of devotees each day who light incense and make offerings of floral garlands. Visitors can witness the grace and beauty of traditional Thai dance performed throughout the day for those who make a donation to the shrine.

# Wat Rachanatdaram and the Loha Prasat

**These pages:** Wat Rachanatdaram is famous for the Loha Prasat or Metal Tower, a square, three-storey construction with 37 spires symbolizing the 37 qualities required to achieve enlightenment in Buddhism. Constructed in 1846, it was modelled on similar temples in India and Sri Lanka. Despite its name, the tower is made from bricks and mortar: only the spires are metal. One 'viham' or temple hall in the compound features an enormous Buddha image (right) and beautiful murals.

# Wat Arun

**These pages:** Wat Arun, known as the Temple of the Dawn, is situated on the banks of the Chao Phraya River. The 79-m (260-ft) Khmer-style chedi is decorated with fragments of porcelain plates and bowls. The temple is particularly beautiful at sunset and can be viewed from the deck of an evening river cruise boat.

# Wat Benchamabophit

*These pages:* Wat Benchamabophit Dusitvanaram is commonly referred to as Wat Ben. It is also known as the Marble Temple because it was constructed in 1899 using Italian Carrara marble. Wat Ben also incorporates other European influences including striking stained-glass windows, rarely seen in Thai temples.

# Assumption Cathedral

**Above:** The original, French-built Assumption Cathedral was constructed during the reign of Rama II in 1821. However, the present Catholic cathedral dates from 1910. Located just off Charoen Krung Road near the Chao Phraya River, it features an elaborate interior and highly decorative ceiling.

# Chapter 3: Historic Bangkok

The city has a rich and fascinating history. Treasures include the encyclopedic riches of the National Museum, the small but equally impressive Jim Thompson House, and the renowned Oriental Hotel. Bangkok also boasts its fair share of monuments and statues honouring former kings and fallen heroes.

## Oriental Hotel

*This page:* The Oriental Hotel is one of the world's most famous hotels. It has been welcoming guests for 150 years. Dignitaries and celebrities have included Somerset Maugham who famously wrote his children's book, 'A Siamese Fairytale', while staying here.

# Jim Thompson House & Museum

**This page:** Jim Thompson House is one of Bangkok's most beautiful museums. The former home of an American military officer who was stationed in Bangkok following World War II, the structure features six traditional teak houses decorated with an outstanding collection of Asian art. Thompson is renowned for helping revitalize Thailand's silk industry and for his mysterious disappearance in Malaysia's Cameroon Highlands on 26th March, 1967 when he left for a walk from which he never returned.

# Democracy Monument

**This page:** Bangkok's Democracy Monument, constructed on Ratchadamnoen Road in 1939, commemorates the coup on 24th June, 1932 that ended the 150-year-old absolute monarchy and introduced a constitutional government to Thailand. Italian sculptor, Corrado Feroci, created the relief sculptures at the base of the monument's four columns.

# Victory Monument

**This page:** Constructed in 1941 under the premiership of Field Marshal Plaek Pibulsongkhram, Victory Monument honours the soldiers, policemen and civilians who sacrificed their lives in a brief conflict between Thailand and France over the demarcation between Thailand and other Indochinese nations. The dispute ended with a compromise being agreed by the two parties, and 59 casualties. Today, Victory Monument acts as a huge traffic island, which is best seen from passing BTS Skytrains.

# Ananta Samakhom Throne Hall

**These pages:** Construction of this grand Renaissance-style building began in 1907 under the orders of Rama V whose statue stands outside. The Ananta Samakhom Throne Hall was designed by Italian architects Mario Tamagno and Annibale Rigotti to be used as a royal assembly hall. The dome of the marble throne hall is covered with picturesque frescoes, but, unfortunately, the interior is now closed to the public.

# The National Museum

**These pages:** Centred on an eighteenth-century palace, the National Museum (top) displays a colossal hoard of the country's artistic riches, ranging from sculptural treasures such as the twelfth-century bronze statue of Boddhisatva Avalokitesvara (below) to exquisite handicrafts. It also houses a highly revered Buddha image, the Phra Buddha Sihing, sitting among the gorgeous murals of the Buddhaisawan Chapel (opposite). All of this is best appreciated on one of the free, weekly, guided tours in English.

# Erawan Museum

**These pages:** The creation of the late Lek Viriyapant, an eccentric business tycoon, the Erawan Museum is crowned by an enormous three-headed elephant. Inside the museum, an elaborate staircase leads to a beautiful stained-glass ceiling. A smaller spiral staircase continues up into the belly of the elephant. There are also a collection of Buddha images and ceramics, and gardens to enjoy.

# Chinatown

**These pages:** Chinatown is one of Bangkok's most historic areas and was originally settled by Chinese traders during the Sukhothai era (1238–1378). According to local superstition, the long winding Yaowarat Road resembles a dragon's body and is therefore an auspicious place to conduct business.

The area includes more than 100 gold shops, businesses selling textiles, antiques and much more. There are also fabulous Chinese restaurants and street stalls, as well as stylish bars and craft-beer pubs. It is a fascinating place to explore in the daytime but takes on a very special atmosphere at night.

Chinese opera, known as 'ngiew' (above) has been
performed in Thailand for more than three centuries. The
colourful shows can be seen in Chinatown throughout Chinese
New Year and on other religious holidays.

# Chapter 4: Everyday Bangkok

Visitors to Bangkok can find moments of peace in welcome green spaces, such as Lumpini and Benjasiri Parks, shop till they drop in palatial malls or experience the vibrancy of colourful markets, including Chatuchak, one of the world's largest. Bangkok also has a lively contemporary arts scene and there are many galleries showcasing local artists.

## Benjasiri Park

**This page:** For its size, Bangkok has very few parks. On central Sukhumvit Road, Benjasiri Park provides a welcome public space for yoga, jogging and playing sports, such as 'takraw', an athletic Asian game of kick volleyball. There are also several sculptures on display.

# Lumpini Park

**This page:** Known as the lungs of Bangkok, this green open space once belonged to Rama VI who gifted it to the people to be used as a public park. It is located on Rama IV Road, between Ratchadamri and Wireless Road with entrance gates on all sides. The park is extremely popular for leisure pursuits and exercise. In the early morning Thai-Chinese gather for Tai Chi, to play traditional board games and to enjoy breakfast together. During the cool season, the Royal Bangkok Symphony Orchestra performs in the park on Sunday afternoons from 5.30 pm.

# Mall Heaven

**These pages:** In recent years, Bangkok has become the home of some of Asia's largest and most ostentatious shopping malls, stocked to the rafters with brand names and luxury goods. Huge malls, such as Siam Paragon, Central World, Icon Siam and The Emporium, are the Buddhist nation's air-conditioned shrines to consumerism. Prime shopping hotspots are concentrated along Sukhumvit Road with direct access from BTS Skytrain stations, so shoppers don't have to brave the traffic. Asiatique (above), is Bangkok's latest riverfront shopping and dining experience.

# Chic bars

**Right:** Over the last twenty years, Bangkok's dining and entertainment scene has enjoyed a renaissance and now offers many chic venues. An evening at a rooftop bar and restaurant for a sundowner with a view is an essential experience. There are several in the city including Red Sky at Centara Grand (shown here), Vertigo and Moon Bar on the 61st floor of the Banyan Tree, the Sky Bar and Sirocco at Lebua, and Belga at Sofitel Bangkok Sukhumvit.

# Art Scene

**This page:** Bangkok's arts scene is blossoming. Bangkok Art and Culture Centre (above) near National Stadium BTS station has several exhibition spaces, a library, shops and restaurants. BACC is one of the hubs for the impressive and wide-ranging Bangkok Art Biennale every two years. Pictured (left) is 'Temporary Insanity', by Pinaree Sanpitak, from the 2023 exhibition, which has silk by Jim Thompson, synthetic fibre, battery, motor, propeller and sound device.

# Khao San Road

**Left:** In the Banglamphu district, a short walk from the Grand Palace and many other historic sites, Khao San Road has a well-deserved reputation as a haven for back-packers. The short but colourful road is lined with stalls selling cheap clothing and jewellery. The area also has an abundance of budget guesthouses and bars.

## Go-Go Bars

**Below:** Bangkok's reputation for spicy nightlife is well deserved. There are several districts in the city such as Pat Pong, Soi Cowboy and Nana with popular go-go bars, and numerous adult massage parlours and bathhouses.

# Chatuchak Market

**Left and right:** On the outskirts of Bangkok, Chatuchak Weekend Market spreads over 14 ha (35 acres) and has over 9,000 stalls selling everything imaginable. Known to Bangkokians as JJ (an abbreviation of the pronunciation of the name), the market is immensely popular and is visited by over 200,000 people every weekend, all in search of a bargain. The market is open every Saturday and Sunday from around 9 a.m. until dusk. When the heat gets too much, there are plenty of places to sit down and enjoy a refreshing drink or lunch.

# Pratunam

**Right:** Open daily, Pratunam Market is renowned as the centre for cheap clothing and fashion accessories. There are three indoor shopping complexes in the area around the Baiyoke Suite Hotel and the side streets are lined with small outlets.

# Pak Khlong Talat

**This page:** Pak Khlong Talat is a colourful market that sells fruit, vegetables and flowers, and offers a vibrant snapshot of Bangkok life. From the early hours of the morning, the market heaves with buyers and sellers. With buckets full of roses and chrysanthemums, and stalls full of fragrant jasmine garlands, it's a colourful sight.

# Phahurat – Little India

**This page:** On the fringes of Chinatown is Phahurat Market, home to Bangkok's minority Indian community. Tucked away down the alleys are some great little restaurants serving authentic Indian food. Phahurat Market is also a good place to buy textiles as most of the community here is involved in the trade.

# Chapter 5: Beyond Bangkok

Several rewarding day trips can be made from Bangkok. The UNESCO World Heritage city of Ayutthaya can be easily reached by train or river boat. Other highlights include cycling in Bang Kra Jao and Koh Kred. There are also floating markets to discover, the fishing town of Mahachai and the country's biggest chedi at Nakhon Pathom.

## Koh Kred

**This page:** Koh Kred is a manmade island in the Chao Phraya River that was originally settled by a community of ethnic Mon from Myanmar who made their living as potters. Once on the island, quiet lanes, temples and potteries can be explored by bicycle. Weekends can be busy with many visitors from Bangkok coming to the island to escape the city and buy pots for their gardens.

# Bang Kra Jao

**This page:** Visit Bang Kra Jao and it's hard to believe you are just a stone's throw from the heart of Bangkok. This undeveloped area is reached by a short boat trip across the Chao Phraya River and can then be explored by bicycle. Over 25 km (15 miles) of pathways wind through the lush green expanse of land past temples and through sleepy villages. Attractions include a weekend floating market and an incense workshop.

# Ayutthaya

**These pages:** A must on any travel itinerary, the UNESCO World Heritage town of Ayutthaya is just 86 km (53 miles) north of Bangkok, making it an ideal destination for a day trip or overnight stay. The town is scattered with ancient temple ruins and imposing Buddha images. From Bangkok, the town can be reached by a leisurely train journey or by a pleasant river cruise. The cruises are offered by several companies and boats usually depart from the pier at the River City Shopping Complex in Bangkok. En route to Ayutthaya the tours stop at Bang Pa-In Summer Palace.

# Mahachai

**These pages:** Just 36 km (22 miles) from Bangkok, the fishing town of Mahachai (Samut Sakhon) makes for an interesting excursion. From the capital it can be reached by a leisurely journey on a train that leaves from Wong Wien Yai station, arriving in the bustling town an hour or so later. Along the Tha Chin River, visitors can watch the fishing boats unload their catch and wander around the busy fresh seafood market.

# Floating Market at Damnoen Saduak

**These pages:** There are several floating markets within easy reach of Bangkok but Damnoen Saduak in Ratchaburi province is the most famous. Located 100 km (62 miles) south-west of Bangkok, the market attracts hundreds of visitors in the early mornings. Despite having genuine origins in the people's waterborne past, today it exists purely as a tourist attraction. However, it is possible to hire a boat and driver to explore a network of other canals in the area and catch a glimpse of a rural life among the palm plantations.

# Nakhon Pathom

***These pages:*** Nakhon Pathom's biggest claim to fame is Phra Pathom Chedi. Founded by Dvaravati Buddhists in the sixth century, the chedi is the tallest Buddhist monument in the world and the oldest in Thailand. The temple surrounding the impressive 127-m (416-foot) chedi is the final resting place of Rama VI. The town is 50 km (31 miles) west of Bangkok.

# Getting About

Bangkok is served by two airports. Suvarnabhumi (pronounced *soo-van-a-poom*) is for both international and domestic flights. Situated approximately 30 km (18 miles) east of central Bangkok, travel time by road is approximately 45 minutes but it also has an elevated rail link to the city centre that takes around 25 minutes. Don Meuang Airport, 24 km (14 miles) north of downtown, operates domestic and Asian international flights. The Dark Red Line elevated train links Don Meuang with Bang Sue, which is on the MRT underground.

In Bangkok, air-conditioned transit systems called the BTS Skytrain and the MRT underground make getting around the city a breeze. Though they don't go everywhere, they stop at many important tourist sites and the system is being extended. The service is fast and efficient. Bangkok has three major bus terminals. Mor Chit serves mostly northern and northeastern destinations. It's located north of Chatuchak Park off Phaholyothin Road. Sai Tai, which serves southern and western destinations, is off Phra Pinklao Road on the western side of the river. Ekamai, at the bottom of Sukhumvit Soi 63, serves eastern destinations. Within the city, buses with air-conditioning cost a little more than those without. All buses, however, can get caught in traffic, so they are not always a good option.

Taxis in Bangkok are readily available around the clock. Meters start at 35 baht and few taxi rides within Bangkok will cost more than 150 baht. Not many drivers speak English, so it's a good idea to have your destination written down in Thai and English. App-based taxi services have recently come to Bangkok, of which the most popular are Grab and Line Man.

*Left:* Opened in 1916, Hua Lampong Station in central Bangkok is a reminder of an age when the train revolutionized travel within Thailand. Today, it's only served by local and stopping trains, while long-distance, express services use the new Krungthep Aphiwat Central Terminal, 8km (5 miles) to the north. Both stations are on the MRT underground system.

*Below:* River taxis ply the Chao Phraya River and the canals.

The ubiquitous three-wheeled *tuk-tuk* is a popular experience for visitors to Bangkok. They do not have a meter and prices should be agreed before starting the journey. Motorcycle taxis are available all over Bangkok and are an essential means of transport if you are in a hurry. They are capable of nipping through the traffic jams and getting you to your destination swiftly. As with *tuk-tuks*, fares must be agreed at the start of the journey. Motorcycle taxi drivers can be identified by their brightly coloured vests with a number on the back.

Boats ply the Chao Phraya River like buses, with fares starting at 14 baht. The piers have maps showing the stops. Most boats have an orange, yellow, red, green or blue flag on their bow indicating which pier they stop at. Longtail boats operate as taxis and can be hired by tourists for sightseeing trips.

*Opposite:* For quick and comfortable travel in Bangkok, the BTS SkyTrain is essential. Value-for-money day passes can be purchased at all stations. The MRT underground is equally efficient. Both networks are continually being expanded.

# Resources

## Contacts

The following websites will provide useful information for organizing your trip.

www.tourismthailand.org

www.tatnews.org

www.bk.asia-city.com

www.timeout.com/bangkok

## Airlines

Thai Airways: www.thaiairways.com

Bangkok Airways: www.bangkokair.com

Nok Air: www.nokair.com

AirAsia: www.airasia.com

Thai Lion Air: www.lion-airthai.com

Viet Jet: www.vietjetair.com

## References

Wyatt, David K. *Thailand: A Short History*. Yale University Press

Phongpaichit, Pasuk and Baker, Chris. *Thailand's Boom and Bust*. Silkworm Books

Ridout, Lucy and Gray, Paul. *The Rough Guide to Bangkok*. Rough Guides

## Acknowledgements

Many thanks to the Princess of Kalasin, Sudarat Ponpangpa, Christian Schlegel of Sofitel Bangkok Sukhumvit, and Prompeth Lertratanapreecha of the Tourist Authority of Thailand.

## About the Author

Mick Shippen is a freelance writer and award-winning photographer who has been based in Southeast Asia for 15 years. He travels extensively throughout Asia conducting research for articles and taking photographs for local and international newspapers and magazines. He is the author of four other titles in this series: *Enchanting Cambodia, Enchanting Laos, Enchanting Thailand* and *Enchanting Myanmar*, and of *The Traditional Ceramics of South East Asia*.

Mick is also a contributing writer for the books *To Asia with Love, To Myanmar with Love,* and *To Thailand with Love*. He has provided content and images for several leading guidebooks, and his work has also appeared in numerous magazines, the *Bangkok Post,* and the Australian *Sunday Telegraph*. His images are represented by Gallery Stock www.gallerystock.com. Images can be viewed at www.mickshippen.com

# Index

Published and Distributed in Thailand by Asia Books Co., Ltd.
88/9 Soi Samanchan-Barbos, Prakanong, Klongtoey, Bangkok 10110, Thailand
Tel: (66) 2-146-599; Email: information@asiabooks.com; www.asiabooks.com

This edition published in the United Kingdom in 2024 by John Beaufoy Publishing,
11 Blenheim Court, 316 Woodstock Road, Oxford OX2 7NS, UK
www.johnbeaufoy.com

ISBN 978-1-913679-69-9

Designed by Glyn Bridgewater
Cover design by Ginny Zeal
Cartography by William Smuts
Project management by Rosemary Wilkinson

Printed and bound in Malaysia by Times Offset (M) Sdn. Bhd

Photo credits
p.6-7 Shutterstock.com/littlewormy, p.14 GOLFX, p.50 top Sombat Muycheen, p.50 bottom Gunawan Kartapranata (cc),
p.51 cowardlion, p.61 Pinaree Sanpitak and Bangkok Art Biennale, p.62 dotmiller1986.

Cover captions:
Front cover: Wat Benchamabophit © Shutterstock/KoBoZaa; Back cover, left to right: A traditional dancer at the
Erawan Shrine; Chinatown; Wat Arun at night; The ubiquitous tuk-tuks, all © Mick Shippen.

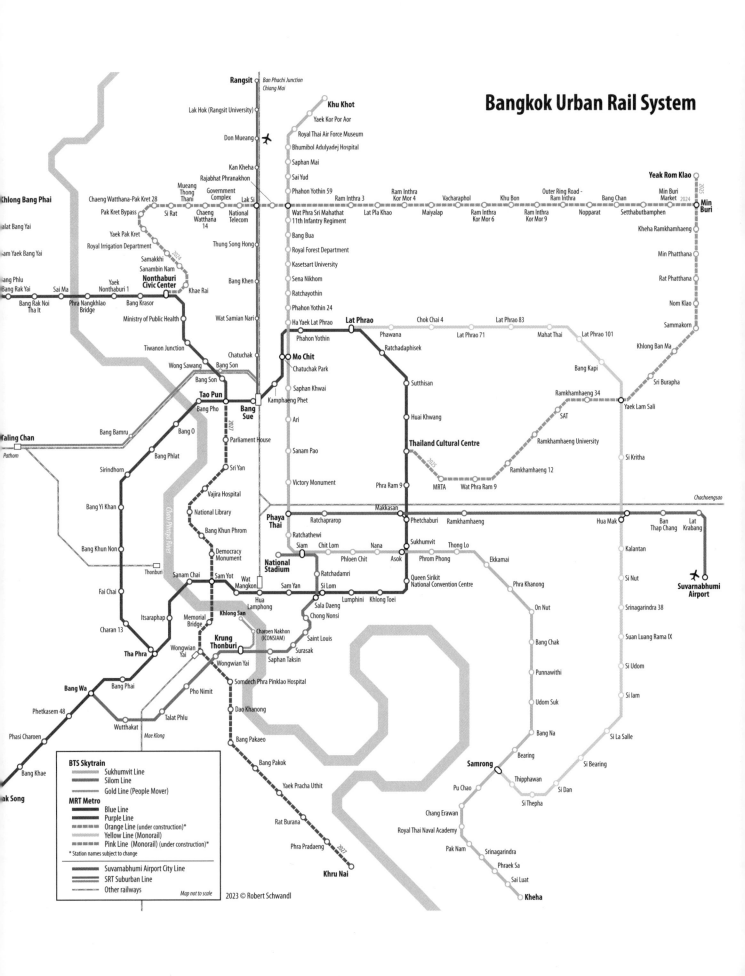

# Bangkok Urban Rail System

**BTS Skytrain**
- Sukhumvit Line
- Silom Line
- Gold Line (People Mover)

**MRT Metro**
- Blue Line
- Purple Line
- Orange Line (under construction)*
- Yellow Line (Monorail)
- Pink Line (Monorail) (under construction)*

*\* Station names subject to change*

- Suvarnabhumi Airport City Line
- SRT Suburban Line
- Other railways

*Map not to scale*

2023 © Robert Schwandl